Sea Poems

Selected by John Foster

First published in the United States of America in 2008 by
dingles & company
P.O. Box 508
Sea Girt, New Jersey 08750

First Printing

Website: www.dingles.com

E-mail: info@dingles.com

Library of Congress Catalog Card No.: 2007907152

ISBN: 978-1-59646-610-4 (library binding)
       978-1-59646-611-1 (paperback)

© Oxford University Press
This U.S. edition of *Sea Poems*, originally published in English in 1990, is published by arrangement with Oxford University Press.

Acknowledgments
The editor and publisher wish to thank the following who have kindly given permission for the use of copyright material:

Finola Akister for "My Castle", © Finola Akister 1990
Moira Andrew for "A Week of August Weather", © Moira Andrew 1988, first published in My Blue Poetry Book: *This Morning my Dad Shouted* (Macmillan Education, 1988)
John Foster for "Sand" and "The Lightship", both © John Foster 1990
Theresa Heine for "Kites", © Theresa Heine 1990
Jean Kenward for "Gulls", © Jean Kenward 1990
John Kitching for "Pebbles", © John Kitching 1990
Sarah Matthews for Stanley Cook: "The Shell", © Stanley Cook 1979, first published in *Word Houses* (1979)
Judith Nicholls for "To the Sea!", © Judith Nicholls 1990
Irene Rawnsley for "At the Seaside", © Irene Rawnsley 1990
Raymond Wilson for "The Lighthouse", © Raymond Wilson 1990

Illustrations by
Stephanie Strickland; Rachel Ross; Katey Farrell; Bucket; Alan Marks; Jill Newton; Jill Barton

Printed in China

∴• dingles &company

Kites

Kites flying,
swoop and sway,
along the beach
on a windy day.

Kites sparkling
like sea spray,
along the beach
on a sunny day.

Kites flapping,
wet and gray,
along the beach
on a rainy day.

Kites tossing,
up and away,
along the beach
on a stormy day.

Theresa Heine

To the Sea!

Who'll be first?
Shoes off,
in a row,
four legs fast,
two legs slow . . .
Ready now?
Off we go!
Tiptoe,
dip-a-toe,
heel and toe –
Yes or no?
Cold as snow!
All at once,
in we go!
One,
   two,
     three,

      SPLASH!

Judith Nicholls

Sand

Sand in your fingernails.
Sand between your toes.
Sand in your earholes.
Sand up your nose.

Sand in your sandwiches.
Sand on your bananas.
Sand in your bed at night.
Sand in your pajamas!

Sand in your sandals.
Sand in your hair.
Sand in your trousers.
Sand everywhere!

John Foster

4

My Castle

It took hours to build my castle
in the sand, the other day.
The tide came in, and in a flash
had washed it all away.

Finola Akister

5

At the Seaside

I walked on the beach
in my brand-new clothes
and stood on the sand
at the edge of the sea
and the sun was shining, shining.

I stepped to the water
on slippery stones
in my brand-new shoes
to search for crabs
in the rock pools shining, shining.

A big wave spilled
and toppled me
in my brand-new clothes
to the cold wet sea
with the pebbles shining, shining.

They brought me home
in my wet-through clothes
to my tucked-up bed
with a brand-new cold
and a sore nose shining, shining.

Irene Rawnsley

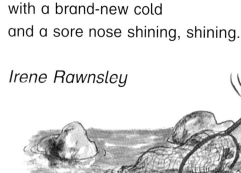

A Week of August Weather

One Saturday when the sun was hot,
we set off for the sea,
my dad, my mom, old Herbert Bear,
my bucket, my shovel – and me.

On Sunday a chilly breeze sprang up
and the sea looked cold and gray.
To keep ourselves warm we hiked the hills –
we went for a *very* long way!

On Monday the rain came pouring down;
we went out and got soaked through.
So we stayed inside all afternoon
and kept wondering what we could do.

On Tuesday morning the sun peeped out
so we raced down to the sea.
By afternoon it was raining once more—
back indoors again long before tea!

9

On Wednesday a soft sea-mist rolled in
making the shore a mysterious place,
and I was glad to hug old Herbert Bear
with his tattered familiar face.

On Thursday lightning lit up the sky
and a storm laced the waves with foam,
so we dodged about from shop to shop
buying presents for people at home.

10

Then Friday dawned a *beautiful* day,
so we paddled and soaked up the sun.
We picnicked, built castles, found dozens
of shells and squeezed in a whole week of fun!

On Saturday the sun was still hot
when we waved good-bye to the sea,
my mom, my dad, old Herbert Bear,
my collection of shells – and me.

Moira Andrew

The Lighthouse

What I remember best about
my vacation was how, each night,
the lighthouse kept sweeping my bedroom
with its clean, cool ray of light.

I lay there, tucked up in the blankets,
and suddenly the lighthouse shone:
a switched-on torch that stabbed the night
with its bright beam and moved on.

Then back it came, out of the dark,
and swung round, as in some fixed plan:
the light of the lighthouse – opening,
folding, and closing like a fan.

Raymond Wilson

The Lightship

The lightship guards the mouth of the bay
to warn other ships to keep away,
to steer clear of the rocky shore
where many a ship has been wrecked before.

Through gales and storms, through day and night,
the lightship flashes its yellow light,
warning sailors to keep away
from the jagged rocks beneath the bay.

John Foster

Pebbles

I pull the pebble from the sand
and hold the pebble in my hand.
It feels so smooth and cool and old.
I dream the stories it's been told –
of princes traveled from distant lands,
of pirates roaming in fierce bands,
of mighty fighting fish and whales,
of savage storms and wrecking gales,
of dead men drowned that tell no tales,
of battleships, of love, of hate,
of fisher-wives who wait and wait.
A million pebbles on the beach
and each its different tale to teach.

John Kitching

The Shell

In winter I put a shell to my ear
and through it I hear
the sound of the sea
answer me.

"Are the donkey and the fair,
boats and gulls still there?
The pier wading out from the land
and starfish like badges on the sand—
will they be there when I come next year?"
The whispering tide
in the shell replies,
"They will all be here
when you come next year."

Stanley Cook

Gulls

I went to the seashore;
I stood upon the sand,
my face to the water,
my back to the land.
I listened to the seagulls,
I heard them call and cry,
They dipped to the water
and soared to the sky.

I went to the seashore,
and nobody was there
except the tossing seagulls
that blew about the air.
I stood, and I watched them,
I heard them cry and call,
with only me to answer
and no one else at all.

Jean Kenward

Space Poems

Selected by John Foster

First published in the United States of America in 2008 by
dingles & company
P.O. Box 508
Sea Girt, New Jersey 08750

First Printing

Website: www.dingles.com

E-mail: info@dingles.com

Library of Congress Catalog Card No.: 2007907152

ISBN: 978-1-59646-610-4 (library binding)
       978-1-59646-611-1 (paperback)

© Oxford University Press
This U.S. edition of *Space Poems*, originally published in English in 1991, is published by arrangement with Oxford University Press.

Acknowledgments
The editor and publisher wish to thank the following who have kindly given permission for the use of copyright material:

Robert Heidbreder: "Space" from *Don't Eat Spiders* (OUP, Canada, 1985), © Robert Heidbreder 1985
Wes Magee for "The Solar System Tour", © Wes Magee 1991
Brian Moses for "Moonbase Classroom Three", © Brian Moses 1991
Paddy Philips for "The Green Man", © Paddy Phillips 1991
Irene Rawnsley for "Space Message", © Irene Rawnsley 1991
Charles Thomson for "Spaceship Race", © Charles Thomson 1991
Raymond Wilson for "From a Space Rocket", © Raymond Wilson 1991
Irene Yates for "Journey into Space", © Irene Yates 1991

Illustrations by
Anthony Rule; Andy Cooke; Nick Sharratt; Alex Brychta; Peet Ellison;
Jan Lewis; Phillippe Dupasquier; Alan Marks

Printed in China

Space

Space is . . .
Planets like Pluto, Jupiter, and Mars;
the Milky Way and billions of stars;
rockets, spaceships, UFOs;
mean, ugly creatures with 36 toes.
Black holes, moons, and solar rays;
dark cold places without any days;
robots, space stations, laser guns;
different galaxies with different suns.

Space is a place I'd love to see
if hungry monsters won't eat me.

Robert Heidbreder

The Solar System Tour

Climb abroad! Yes, climb aboard!
You'll have a lifetime's thrill!
You'll love the Solar System tour.
We know, we *know* you will!

We'll whizz you right around Saturn,
then Mercury, then Mars!
See Venus, and see Neptune!
You'll spot six million stars!

Jupiter and Uranus!
Pluto! Our Earth and Moon!
So, climb aboard the spaceship!
Be quick! We're leaving soon!

Wes Magee

Journey into Space

We went on a journey
a journey, a journey.
We went in a rocket,
Jaswinder and me.
We went past the moon
and we went past the planets.
We sailed into Sunspace,
Jaswinder and me.
We landed at daybreak
at daybreak, at daybreak.
We landed in secret,
Jaswinder and me.
Then the aliens found us
and danced all around us
and made plans to crown us,
Jaswinder and me.
But we climbed in our rocket,
our rocket, our rocket,
and zoomed back to earth,
just in time for our tea.

Irene Yates

21

Moonbase Classroom Three

This is Moonbase classroom three
and we're spending Christmas in Space.
We never thought we'd finish in time;
it's really been quite a race.

We've made an effort for Christmas;
strung paper chains from the stars,
while Santa Claus in full space gear
is steering a course for Mars.

We think this must be the first time
anyone's partied on the moon.
"What about weightlessness?" we ask.
"Would jelly stay on the spoon?"

Our teacher says, after vacation
we'll be starting on something new,
but robots and moon shots are much more fun
than anything else we might do.

It's seldom that something we've done at school
has ever been so much fun.
We've really been over the moon
and the planets, the stars, and the sun!

Brian Moses

23

Spaceship Race

Look, look,
it's the spaceship race –
Mars to Jupiter.
What a pace!
Rockets whizzing
all over the place.

Whizz whizz!
Whoosh whoosh!
One's broken down –
give it a push.

Red's in front,
Green's behind,
Blue's blown up
(never mind).

Green goes faster,
Yellow's overtaken.
Green's going to win
if I'm not mistaken.

Green's going to win –
I bet you my dinner.
Green's going to
.... oh no!
Red is the winner.

Charles Thomson

The Green Man

A spaceship's in my garden.
It landed there last night.
It's very round and shiny.
It did give me a fright.
But when I called this morning,
the door was opened wide,
and to my great amazement,
a green man stepped outside.
He really was unusual,
so very, very small.
In fact, he was so tiny he
was hardly there at all.

He greeted me politely,
and kindly was his plea
to "Come right in, and welcome
to a cup of Martian tea."
I had green bread and butter,
with green jam on the bread.
I could have had green pancakes
but chose green buns instead.

I said, "I'd better leave now,"
for time was speeding by.
He said, "Of course, by all means,
for I, too, now must fly."
While I watched rather sadly,
the spaceship flew away.
Our garden seemed so empty,
and suddenly, the day.

I've just looked in the mirror.
It's plain where I have been,
for when I put my tongue out,
I noticed it was green.

Paddy Phillips

29

Space Message

A spaceman
flew down from his distant kingdom
bringing a message
from one of the stars.

He stood in the street
in his garment of silver;
he shone on the houses,
he shone on the cars.

He shone in the faces of people
who listened;
they all closed their eyes,
but they heard what he said.

"Take care of your earth,
look after its creatures.
Don't leave your children
a planet that's dead!"

Irene Rawnsley

From a Space Rocket

We looked back at the World
    rolling through Space
like a giant Moon with a calm
    cool silver face.

All its cities and countries
    had faded from sight;
all its mountains and oceans were turned
    into pure light.

Slowly, its noise and troubles
    all seemed to cease,
and the whole World was beauty and silence
    and endless peace.

Raymond Wilson